Dedication & Acknowledgments

To those who desire to enter through the narrow gate: May your fruit bring glory and honor to God, and may your pruning seasons draw you closer to the One you love.

To my husband, thank you for always supporting me and showing me what a covenant marriage looks like.

To my kids, may you be marked by God and bear much fruit for His Kingdom and His Glory.

Fruit in the Field

ISBN - 978-1-952840-90-6
UNITED HOUSE Publishing Clarkston, Michigan
info@unitedhousepublishing.com www.unitedhousepublishing.com

Interior Design: Talitha McGuinness;
talitha@unitedhousepublishing.com
Printed in the United States of America 2026 - First Edition

SPECIAL SALES:
Most UNITED HOUSE books are available at special quantity discounts when purchased in bulk by corporations, organizations, and special interest groups. For more information, please email orders@unitedhousepublishing.com.

List of Contents

Fruit in the Field

Introduction to Part I:
By Their Fruit You Will Recognize Them

By their fruit you will recognize them. Do people pick grapes from thornbushes, or figs from thistles? Likewise, every good tree bears good fruit, but a bad tree bears bad fruit. A good tree cannot bear bad fruit, and a bad tree cannot bear good fruit. Every tree that does not bear good fruit is cut down and thrown into the fire. Thus, by their fruit you will recognize them.
Matthew 7:16-20, NIV

We are designed to bear good fruit; fruit in keeping with the scriptures. The Lord's heart for us in bearing fruit is not that we'd be impressed by full branches but that we'd be solely focused on the One who sustains us. He desires that our attachment to the Vine would be more significant than the fruit itself, and that our hearts and lives would not find fulfillment in what is blooming but in what feeds us.

To bear fruit is simply to live a life that reproduces the values, characteristics, and traits of Jesus Christ. The fruit we bear is highly connected to what is happening spiritually in our lives; they go hand in hand. Godly fruit is a byproduct of the work of the Spirit in us through refining, shaping, and obedience. The question we must answer is: Does the fruit we produce grow on the tree of life or the tree of death? Is it the fruit of God and His Son Jesus, or of Satan? No matter where the Lord places you, your fruit will be seen by many. In how you live, what you speak about or withhold from speaking about, how you serve, and how you steward your finances.

As we jump into these pages, there's no preparation required—just a present decision to ask God the Father, Christ the Son, and the Holy Spirit to search your heart. I pray that He will reveal to you the fruit you are bearing in His name, as well as that which is not. One thing you may not have been aware of is that your life is already producing fruit. May I ask you, which kind?

Fruit in the Field

PART I

GOOD FRUIT

Fruit in the Field

CHAPTER ONE: Where Fruit All Began

Then God said, 'Let the land produce vegetation: seed-bearing plants and trees on the land that bear fruit with seed in it, according to their various kinds.' And it was so.
Genesis 1:11, NIV

So God created the great creatures of the sea and every living thing with which the water teems and that moves about in it, according to their kinds, and every winged bird according to its kind. And God saw that it was good. God blessed them and said, 'Be fruitful and increase in number and fill the water in the seas, and let the birds increase on the earth.'
Genesis 1:21-22, NIV

*So God created mankind in his own image,
in the image of God he created them;
male and female he created them.
God blessed them and said to them, 'Be fruitful and increase in number; fill the earth and subdue it. Rule over the fish in the sea and the birds in the sky and over every living creature that moves on the ground.'*
Genesis 1:27-28, NIV

We see three times, on days three, five, and six, how God blessed what was made and told it to bear fruit, to multiply. When He says to multiply, it's essential to note that He's not just instructing us to multiply a physical human or plant, but to multiply the nature of God.

The Tree in the Middle

Scripture states Eve was tempted by the serpent in the garden. The serpent was crafty, twisting and manipulating God's Word.

God: And the Lord God commanded the man, 'You are free to eat from any tree in the garden; but you must not eat from the tree of the knowledge of good and evil, for when you eat from it you will certainly die' (Genesis 2:16-17, NIV).

Satan: He said to the woman, "Did God really say, 'You must not eat from any tree in the garden'" (Genesis 3:1, NIV)?

In his very wording, Satan is both confusing and misleading. He's almost implying they could eat from any of the trees. There's no clear indication of one tree. In contrast, God said you can eat from *any* of the trees, but I've advised against the tree of the knowledge of good and evil because the consequence is death. Notice how God states the tree is the tree of the knowledge of good and evil.

Eve answers the serpent, saying, "It's the tree in the middle." This response intrigues me because, instead of explaining why God instructed Adam to avoid the tree, she simply mentioned its location. It serves as a reminder that we must reflect on the reasons behind God's commands and their significance. Rather than recalling the concepts of good and evil, or even the warning "you will die," she focused solely on where the tree was. While her statement may have been factually correct, it overlooked the deeper reason why God warned Adam—and by extension, her—to stay away.

Satan used the fruit to tempt Eve, and she and Adam gave in to it. They had their eyes opened and ultimately covered themselves because they realized they were naked. When Eve handed the fruit to Adam, we witnessed the first sin passed down within a family— wife to husband, then to their son, Cain, and to generations to come.

In the Garden, the tree of the knowledge of good and evil grew alongside the trees with good fruit—fruit that could sustain Adam and Eve. This is important to note because both types of fruit can co-exist. There can be edible glorifying-to-God fruit growing beside fruit that will enslave, poison, and eventually kill us.

Redeeming What's Been Stolen
The fruit's reputation is tied to sin entering the world. By eating

it, an environment of evil, fear, and insecurity entered the picture. So why is it that God has still chosen to use bearing fruit and fruit itself as an indication of life and health? Why did He not just deem it "bad" because of what happened and interchange the words with "emulate Jesus," "make good decisions," or "do the right things?" I don't know the actual answer; I'm not God. But I do believe God created the words "fruit" and "bearing fruit" as a sign of His favor and blessing (Deuteronomy 28).

God is redeeming what Satan tried to steal in the Garden. He has shown us this through Jesus coming to die for our sins. We have access to Him through our belief in His Son. Our very salvation is God allowing us to return to where it all began with no separation, no coverings, and no space between us and Him. God has chosen to take the very thing we should feel a sense of shame about—fruit—to glorify Himself.

Know that God has put you here to bear fruit. Not just a little fruit, but an abundance for His Kingdom and His name. He's given us the ability to grow life-giving fruit alongside deadly fruit. It's our responsibility, based on the Word of God and the prompting of the Holy Spirit, to distinguish between them.

At times in our lives, He's telling us not to eat a particular fruit to caution us, for we may come to crave it and eventually reproduce it. The danger with reproducing bad fruit is that it's not just inedible, but it also takes over land which was always intended to be filled with God's fruit.

Be encouraged, friend, that God is a master redeemer, and even if the fruit you see isn't of Him, He can remove and replant. He can uproot and tear down. Nothing is too hard for our God!

Fruit in the Field

CHAPTER TWO: Separation

For God said, 'If they face war, they might change their minds and return to Egypt.'
Exodus 13:17, NIV

One reason the Israelites were at the Red Sea was that God had led them a long way to where they were going. Taking a longer path, at times, is a necessary tool of the Father. There can be protection in the long path. It separates us from old, sinful habits and, at times, from people. The long way, although uncomfortable and often undesirable, is where we learn the nature of our Father. We learn to hear His voice more clearly and to wait until He says to move. The Israelites sought both freedom and familiarity. These don't often go hand in hand. Without the detour, they'd run back to their old ways.

God knew they would likely return to Egypt, slavery, and bondage in exchange for war. The idea or illusion of opposition was strong enough to nullify the Father's good works. When God calls us into marking seasons—where He divinely separates us and sets us apart—there is great room for the voice of the enemy to increase and our minds to run wild with lies. It's imperative that we continually be transformed in our minds and guard ourselves with the word of God during these seasons. We mustn't grow weary or faint, but we must seek His word now more than ever and pray more fervently.

One definition of separation is *division*. This implies that a clear boundary is necessary so there is no crossing; the two things can't mix. It's

*but those who hope in the Lord will renew their strength.
They will soar on wings like eagles;
they will run and not grow weary,
they will walk and not be faint.*
Isaiah 40:31, NIV

easy to want God to use us or separate us without having to endure complications or hardship. God may have you in a period where you feel like you're going through hardship, or maybe you don't feel like there's much fruit being birthed. Let me encourage you that His timing is perfect and the process is intentional. He sometimes has to do things the hard way —the longer way —but, most importantly, the lasting way. He hasn't brought you to a Red Sea moment to drown you, or because you've been bad. He's got you at the Red Sea because He needs to show you who He is so that you can step into His provision.

Pharaoh will think, 'The Israelites are wandering around the land in confusion, hemmed in by the desert.' And I will harden Pharaoh's heart, and he will pursue them. But I will gain glory for myself through Pharaoh and all his army, and the Egyptians will know that I am the Lord.
Exodus 14:3-4, NIV

God's decision to change Pharaoh's heart was for His own glory. Without Pharaoh's pursuit of the Israelites, there would never have been a need for a Red Sea moment. As much as God wanted to show the Egyptians He was the one true God, I believe He also wanted to show His great love for His people.

Then the angel of God, who had been traveling in front of Israel's army, withdrew and went behind them. The pillar of cloud also moved from in front and stood behind them, coming between the armies of Egypt and Israel. Throughout the night the cloud brought darkness to one side and light to the other side; so neither went near the other all night long.
Exodus 14:19-20, NIV

He created a protective barrier as they traveled through the night. He lit the way for them along the path through the Red Sea. As they reached dry ground on the other side of the Red Sea at daybreak, He had Moses stretch out his hand over the sea to close it up. They watched chariots and men drown before their very eyes. Imagine the joy and excitement you'd have; imagine the freedom you'd instantly feel in the moment. It would cause you not only to praise God but also to understand that His hand was truly upon you.

The Mind

Even though this moment was significant, the Israelites would spend many years wandering in the desert because they struggled to remove the remnants of Egypt from their minds completely. Was part of the reason God killed the Egyptians so they didn't have an option to go back?

Romans 12:2 ESV tells us, "Do not be conformed to this world, but be transformed by the renewal of your mind, that by testing you may discern what is the will of God, what is good and acceptable and perfect." Living a separated life requires a renewal of the mind. It demands that we maintain a fixed focus on Heaven and what is eternal, rather than on what is before us. The things of this world are not to entice us—they're not even to hold our affection.

To be marked as one separated for the Lord is a great gift. It is not one to be taken lightly. It means that He deems you worthy to not only carry your cross but also to submit to His very call. This is a narrow and costly road, my friend, but it is a fruitful one. It is full of eternal

Don't despise the times when God removes things from your life. His heart is always filled with a desire to love and free us. I feel the Holy Spirit saying that some people reading this have been bitter and angry because God has asked for things in their finances and with their time. You don't think it's the best thing for you. You want to go your own way. But your own way will lead to bondage and slavery. He is presenting a NEW and BETTER way. Don't look back to Egypt. It has the illusion of protection or understanding, but it only seeks to enslave you.

rewards to be reaped one day. This is because our focus is not on what is but instead on what is to come.

The fruit of separation is a heart and life submitted to the Father's will. It will entail sacrifice and trusting God's voice above all else. It looks like Abraham, Esther, Ruth, Joshua, David, Deborah, Paul, and Jesus. It is a pleasing aroma unto the Lord because it is reminiscent of His Son, not the flesh.

> *For many are invited,*
> *but few are chosen.*
> Matthew 22:14, NIV

CHAPTER THREE: Humility

Come to Me, all you who are weary and burdened, and I will give you rest. Take My yoke upon you and learn from me; for I am gentle and humble in heart, and you will find rest for your souls. For My yoke is easy and My burden is light.
Matthew 11:28-30, NIV

Jesus is the ultimate example of humility. He desired to humble Himself to glorify the Father more fully. True humility is nurtured when we value Jesus above ourselves and surrender our lives, desires, and will in exchange for His. Humility is not focused on self but on fulfilling the will of the Father.

In the Book of Ruth, we see the fruit of humility time and time again. Ruth is willing to set her physical and emotional needs aside to meet others' needs. She does not stop to be seen and does not grumble during the harsh labor she undergoes. Her eyes are fixed; her life is laid down, and because of it, she bears a harvest greater than she could have imagined.

<u>Clinging</u>

Ruth married one of Naomi's sons, Mahlon. He, along with his brother and father, died while they lived in Moab. Naomi, who was from Judah, relinquished her daughters-in-law so that they could return home to their own gods and families. She even blessed them along the way: "At this, they wept aloud again. Then Orpah kissed her mother-in-law goodbye, but Ruth clung to her" (Ruth 1:14, NIV). We see here that Orpah returned to what she knew —her family and comfort —while Ruth clung to Naomi.

Ruth couldn't imagine leaving Naomi. She was her family, and there was a love there that ran deep. To Orpah, returning to what she knew was what she desired. A foreign land, a foreign God, everything was just too much for Orpah to commit to. She loved Naomi, but there was a limit to her love.

Ruth was willing to lay down what felt comfortable and what she knew. This was not only to return with Naomi but to serve her. One definition of humility is freedom from pride or arrogance, not thinking of yourself as better than other people.[1] Ruth exemplified this over and over again in the scriptures. Her humility wasn't showy; instead, it was quiet and private, allowing people to see and experience it through her actions.

Unoffendable

Ruth's fruit of humility begins to mature throughout chapters 2 and 3 in the book of Ruth. Over and over again in the scriptures, Ruth decides to serve with humility.

And Ruth the Moabite said to Naomi, 'Let me go to the fields and pick up the leftover grain behind anyone in whose eyes I find favor.'
Ruth 2:2, NIV

So she went out, entered a field and began to glean behind the harvesters.
Ruth 2:3, NIV

At this, she bowed down with her face to the ground. She asked him, "Why have I found such favor in your eyes that you notice me— a foreigner?
Ruth 2:10, NIV

So Ruth gleaned in the field until evening. Then she threshed the barley she had gathered, and it amounted to about an ephah. She carried it back to town, and her mother-in-law saw how much she had gathered. Ruth also brought out and gave her what she had left over after she had eaten enough.
Ruth 2:17-18, NIV

Not only does she go to the fields, but she also gleans behind the harvesters. Gleaning at that time was often designated for people experiencing poverty, widows, and orphans.

Ruth is not offended by her position behind others. It doesn't cause her to demand a better position as she gleans, nor even to grumble. Ruth remains grateful in her heart posture and is actively worshiping God through her submission to the yoke He had for her at that moment.

At times, God will take us through periods of humbling, often filled with repentance and an exposure of our sins we have not dealt with or are unaware of. What is your posture with the Lord when you enter into these times? Is it "Get me out of here!" or is it a posture of "Thank you, Lord Jesus, for showing this to me. I repent?" It's easy to become offended or upset with situations God will use to humble us because our flesh is loud. It screams for attention and often is arrogant enough to think it knows what's best for us. Have you been allowing God's humbling, gentle hand to offend you? Has it caused you to retreat from your relationship or intimacy with Him?

> *Do not go over your vineyard a second time or pick up the grapes that have fallen. Leave them for the poor and the foreigner. I am the LORD your God.*
> Leviticus 19:10, NIV

> *When you are harvesting in your field and you overlook a sheaf, do not go back to get it. Leave it for the foreigner, the fatherless and the widow, so that the LORD your God may bless you in all the work of your hands. When you beat the olives from your trees, do not go over the branches a second time. Leave what remains for the foreigner, the fatherless and the widow. When you harvest the grapes in your vineyard, do not go over the vines again. Leave what remains for the foreigner, the fatherless and the widow. Remember that you were slaves in Egypt. That is why I command you to do this.*
> Deuteronomy 24:19-22, NIV

Fruit in the Field

Ruth is unoffended and worshipful during one of her life's toughest and possibly loneliest seasons. She isn't just without a spouse but is also in a foreign land she has never been to before, living as a servant. Worshipping God isn't merely limited to our words in song; it is more often than not the posture of our lives. One of the greatest gifts we receive is the opportunity to worship God in the midst of hardship. We get to double down and not only worship Him in song but with lips that refuse to grumble or complain about our circumstances, in steady hands desiring to serve God regardless of the current situation, and with feet fixated on being where God desires to plant them, even if it is humbling.

Ruth's fruit of humility reflects the greatest commandments about which Jesus spoke to the religious leaders.

Jesus replied: 'Love the Lord your God with all your heart and with all your soul and with all your mind.' This is the first and greatest commandment. And the second is like it: 'Love your neighbor as yourself.' All the Law and the Prophets hang on these two commandments.
Matthew 22:37-40, NIV

She was living out the commands before Jesus ever spoke them. The fruit Ruth bore over and over again was the fruit of humility. Humility is not a one-time decision or act; it is a conscious effort to live your life submitted to God daily above yourself. When we fail to humble ourselves before God and treat ourselves as the ultimate authority in our lives, it allows sins like pride and arrogance to take root in our hearts. These two combat the fruit of humility springing forth in us.

What would it take for you and me to live a humble life? What would we have to give up that we are currently clinging to? If you have realized that you are living a life that doesn't bear the fruit of humility, I would encourage you not only to repent before God but also to give Him authority and access to correct and rebuke you. He will do it most kindly and gently.

CHAPTER FOUR: Resilience

*Then Jesus was led by the Spirit into the wilderness to be tempted
by the devil. After fasting forty days and forty nights, he was
hungry. The tempter came to Him and said, 'If you are the Son
of God, tell these stones to become bread.' Jesus answered, 'It is
written: 'Man shall not live on bread alone, but on every word
that comes from the mouth of God.' Then, the devil took Him to
the holy city and had Him stand on the highest point of the temple.
'If you are the Son of God,' he said, 'throw yourself down. For it is
written: "He will command his angels concerning you, and they
will lift you up in their hands, so that you will not strike your foot
against a stone."' Jesus answered him, "It is also written: 'Do not
put the Lord your God to the test.' Again, the devil took Him to
a very high mountain and showed Him all the kingdoms of the
world and their splendor. 'All this I will give you,' he said, 'if you
will bow down and worship me.'Jesus said to him, 'Away from me,
Satan! For it is written: 'Worship the Lord your God, and serve
Him only.'" Then the devil left Him,
and angels came and attended Him.*
Matthew 4:1-11, NIV, emphasis added

No Resilience Without Testing

The Spirit of the living God led Jesus into His period of testing. This is often not spoken about among Christians. In fact, when faced with a test or trial, we often desire to pray our way out of the situation, avoiding what God is using to refine us into His own image. The fruit of resilience requires testing and temptation. It is impossible to be resilient if there is nothing that presses us or offers us the opportunity to fail. Part of walking in relationship with our Savior is having a spirit that knows that pressing is part of our walk with Him, from glory to glory. There must be testing to determine if we can responsibly handle the weight of the glory He wants to bestow on us. His glory is costly and valuable. And He's such a kind God that He wouldn't give us something intentionally that we are not mature enough to handle.

Combatting Weapon

Each time Jesus is tempted, He responds with the Word of God. He doesn't answer apart from that which has already been breathed since the foundations of the world. When testing and tempting enter your life, what do you use as your combatting weapon?

While scripture points us to many things, such as prayer, petitioning, being clothed in the armor of God, fasting, and other spiritual disciplines, the Word from which we draw these truths is the weapon. I have responded to the enemy during times of warfare with my perspective on the situation or with half-truths about God, rather than using the Word of God as the source. I get caught in the physical, trying to fight the eternal. The beautiful thing about the Word of God is that it transcends. This means it can serve as a mechanism of hope and remembrance for you, while at the same time retreating the enemy, reminding him of his lack of authority and dominion. It is a double-edged sword.

Be Encouraged

Be encouraged, friend, for the Lord longs to refresh us in times of difficulty. He longs for us to lie down in green pastures and rest. The Lord longs for us to sit at the table He prepared before our enemies. Why? Because by leaning into Him, we are trusting Him as our provider. He isn't merely a God to whom we throw prayer requests or a list of demands. He transitions from a "quiet time" God to an "every moment of the day, I desire your presence" God. He longs for us to hold fast to Him, and times of difficulty unfortunately draw this out of us.

> *Father, if you are willing, take this cup from me; yet not my will, but yours be done.*
> Luke 22:42, NIV

Jesus shows us His deep love for the Father over and over again in Scripture. But these particular verses found in Matthew 4:1-11 are so sweet. The Savior of the world chose to agree with His Father's will and submit, even if it cost Him physically. It's as though Jesus's simple obedience to the movement of the Spirit in the desert and throughout His life communicates something far more significant.

> *By myself I can do nothing; I judge only as I hear, and my judgment is just, for I seek not to please myself but him who sent me.*
> John 5:40, NIV

He's saying, "I will not avoid tests, trials, or hardship because this life is not about me. God, you have my 'yes' even if it costs me something. If you're there in the desert, that's where I want to be. If you're there in the lashings, that's where I want to be. If you're there on the cross, that's where I want to be."

The physical opposition and hardship don't even compare to the glory or love He has for you. So run towards the seed of resilience, as it's one of the most significant ways you can worship Him. He will never leave or forsake you there. It's His promise.

Fruit in the Field

CHAPTER FIVE: Maturity

In fact, though by this time you ought to be teachers, you need someone to teach you the elementary truths of God's word all over again. You need milk, not solid food! Anyone who lives on milk, being still an infant, is not acquainted with the teaching about righteousness. But solid food is for the mature, who by constant use have trained themselves to distinguish good from evil.
Hebrews 5:12-14, NIV

We don't like to identify with or even acknowledge that there could be a deficiency in our lives. Something about the word just rubs us the wrong way. But whether we want to say it or not, it is very prevalent these days. In the Book of Hebrews, we get a clear warning about what it looks like to have a deficiency in the faith or be malnourished in the faith.

Maturity Check Up
The author of Hebrews is unknown, but Paul, Luke, Barnabas, and Priscilla have been suggested as possible authors. What they're trying to communicate is that there is a massive gap in the Jewish-Christians' spiritual maturity at the time. The people should have moved past the elementary teaching of Christ, yet they were stuck in a cycle. They should've been teaching and spreading the gospel, but they were stagnant.

Far too often, Christians who claim to have known the Lord for years have only experienced a small part of Him. They gave their life to Christ, started serving, and joined a group. In their heads, they've checked the boxes. And if this is you, don't feel bad. I was once there. I had a limited perspective of God in my life and a hardened heart that was glued to its own comfort, control, and plan. He could be part of my life, but not have ALL of my life. I wanted to have a relationship with God, but it would have to fit in a particular way. He would need to fit the molds I'd been taught or things I had drawn up about Him. I was drinking milk, trying to shape the God of the Universe into my own image. I was walking in the basics of my faith, unwilling to step out and mature.

Here are some maturity checks I've seen in my own life.
1. Are you and your desires the center of your prayer life, or is exalting Him the center of your prayer life?
2. Is God the Lord of your life, or is something or someone else sitting on the throne of your heart?
3. If God came tomorrow and asked you for something, would He already have your yes?
4. Have you willingly laid your life down for Christ? Would you physically be willing to die for him?
5. Does your relationship with Jesus permeate your whole day, or is it confined to specific times and windows (i.e., quiet time, prayer time)?

<u>Look Like Jesus</u>

For many of us, following God is a concept, not a belief. It stems from an understanding, not a relationship. We understand from a scriptural perspective that there is one God and He sent His Son, Jesus, to die for us, but it often remains in the mind, never transitioning fully to the heart. While we have great intentions in mind when we give our lives to Christ, we can find ourselves slipping into a "do this for me" relationship with God. We look more towards what we can benefit from rather than what we are to lose.

The word "Christian" comes from Christ's name, thus indicating we should strive to embody or reflect Christ's nature. My life, actions, time, finances, and heart should reflect the same things Christ does. If you were to examine your life, what parts would not look like the Jesus you read about in your Bible?

Jesus, who loved His neighbors and enemies. Jesus, who would regularly put His needs to the side to meet others. Jesus, who would rise early to go and be alone with the Father. Jesus, who was unattached to things of this world. Maturity in our walks with Christ will require that we graduate past the rudimentary understanding of our faith.

I believe God desires for His people to crave Him and enter into a mature, fulfilling relationship with Him—one not focused on us, but on Him and His Lordship in our lives. He desires that we would no longer be satisfied with mere liquids, but eager to chew. That the reward of knowing Him more intimately would outweigh the cost of following.

> *I gave you milk, not solid food, for you were not yet ready for it.*
> *Indeed, you are still not ready.*
> 1 Corinthians 3:2, NIV

God is an abundant God. He wants to give you and me more than milk and honey. His table is full of every good thing —so why should we settle for liquids?

The sadness about being malnourished as a believer is that our faith in God will never increase. It remains stagnant. His identity becomes wrapped in how we once experienced Him. We focus on how He once moved, how He once spoke. If there's anything I know, it's that God is the same yesterday, today, and tomorrow. But how God moves changes daily, moment by moment.

The enemy wants you to have a narrow view of who God is and can be. He wants us to see Him as a routine, simple God. He wants our sight to be limited to only see the milk and honey before us, but there is so much more God offers. For decades, he has been robbing the Body of Christ of sitting at the table full of a bounty of fresh food. Chewable, healthy food.

For far too long, we have been distracted by things that will burn in Heaven and be viewed by the Father as a mismanagement of our time and efforts. Jesus is coming back for a pure, spotless, and righteous bride. He longs to meet us, in all our glory, standing undefiled before Him. Maturity and righteousness are the way of the bride. This is why the road is narrow.

If you feel the Spirit prompting you to sow seeds of maturity or righteousness in your relationship with Him, please don't resist. I know it feels costly, even wildly difficult. But He knows the way and is waiting for you, His pure bride. Do you hear the wedding bells?

CHAPTER SIX: Truth

Then the herald loudly proclaimed, 'Nations and peoples of every language, this is what you are commanded to do: As soon as you hear the sound of the horn, flute, zither, lyre, harp, pipe and all kinds of music, you must fall down and worship the image of gold that King Nebuchadnezzar has set up. Whoever does not fall down and worship will immediately be thrown into a blazing furnace.'
Daniel 3:4-6, NIV

The story of Shadrach, Meshach, and Abednego is one of boldness. In the book of Daniel, we're introduced to these three men standing up for truth in the midst of a crowd that is bowing down to the demands of an earthly king. Nebuchadnezzar erected a gold statue of himself and summoned all the people to worship his image.

To not obey the king's command was to accept death by fire. These three Jewish youths decided not to bow down and were brought before the King. What ensued was full of the fruit of truth.

Now when you hear the sound of the horn, flute, zither, lyre, harp, pipe and all kinds of music, if you are ready to fall down and worship the image I made, very good. But if you do not worship it, you will be thrown immediately into a blazing furnace. Then what god will be able to rescue you from my hand?

Shadrach, Meshach and Abednego replied to him, 'King Nebuchadnezzar, we do not need to defend ourselves before you in this matter. If we are thrown into the blazing furnace, the God we serve is able to deliver us from it, and He will deliver us from Your Majesty's hand. But even if He does not, we want you to know, Your Majesty, that we will not serve your gods or worship the image of gold you have set up.'
Daniel 3:15-18, NIV

Don't Let Intimidation Corrupt the Truth

These men are being intimidated into following the crowd. They are challenged and tested to see if they will conform to what they don't believe. The threat of death had many bowing their heads. If we are willing to abandon our relationship with the Lord when presented with hardship or death, do we actually believe in God as we say we do? Not standing up here would be to deny the truth of God altogether. God wasn't looking for them to say, "Well, I believe you in my heart." He wanted to know if they'd be willing to stand boldly and say, "I believe in God publicly."

It can be easy for Christians to live private lives with Christ and public lives that are unintentionally bowed down to the world. Submitting to and acknowledging Him in private is easy, but if it's going to cost how they look before peers or family, well, that's too costly. God is looking for a remnant of people who are so anchored in the truth of the Word of God that they know they don't owe anyone an explanation for why they will not bow. The fire does not threaten them because they long to please their Father.

Where Are You Pulling Your Truth From?

The fruit these men produced was truth. They exposed the truth to a whole group of people who had either dwindled in their faith in Yahweh or who didn't know His name. May I ask you a personal question—where do you find the truth? What does truth look like to you? I think it's important to be honest with yourself when answering this question and not give a generic response.

Truth is what we operate out of. Truth isn't a concept or an idea I hold; no, it is the place from which I make decisions. It's possible to know the truth and not live the truth. This may be why Jesus says, "Many will say to me on that day, 'Lord, Lord, did we not prophesy in Your name and in Your name drive out demons and in Your name perform many miracles?' Then I will tell them plainly, 'I never knew you. Away from me, you evildoers!'" (Matthew 7:22-23, NIV).

I've witnessed people take Fox News or CNN News and what they're reporting as their place of truth over the Bible. Instead of loving their neighbor, as the Word of God tells us to, their truth becomes whatever someone tells them. And in a society where the word "truth" has become merely an expression of one's personal belief, ungoverned by God's authority, we must be aware that the basis of our definition is imperative.

There is only one true thing, and that's the Bible. Thus, there is only one truth, the word of God. It doesn't alter itself to meet your preferences or views. It doesn't relinquish its authority to make you feel like you have more. It corrects, proves, heals, and restores. The Bible is the truth.

The fruit of truth may rub up against people the wrong way. It will make people feel uncomfortable. It challenges their sin. It exposes the heart's true motives. But the truth is our most valuable asset. It's more important than retirement accounts, IRAs, insurance, or our families. We have a huge truth deficit. We have littered our minds with a million versions of false truth, struggling to cling to or acknowledge the only absolute truth: the Word of God. Do you believe in the truth of the Bible? Not just parts of it, but the whole thing?

<u>Are You Embracing the Fire?</u>
"Shadrach, Meshach and Abednego, and these three men, firmly tied, fell into the blazing furnace."
Daniel 3:23, NIV

"He said, "Look! I see four men walking around in the fire, unbound and unharmed, and the fourth looks like a son of the gods."
Daniel 3:25, NIV

Scripture says they were firmly tied and fell into the furnace. This is a stark contrast to the two verses later that follow, which say they were walking around unbound. Fire tests the truth.

The fire was as much for Nebuchadnezzar as it was for Shadrach,

Meshach, and Abednego. It demonstrated both the power of God and the truth of His Word, revealing that He is the one true God. If you feel like you're sitting in a fire right now or like you're about to be thrown into one, please know He's with you. The fire is not intended to cause us to be fearful or to run, but it is there to get us to see the truth, or lack thereof, we are standing on. Sometimes, we are unaware until the threat of fire challenges us.

God was with Shadrach, Meshach, and Abednego when they didn't bow down, just as much as when they were in the furnace. The Lord's provision never wavered. He is unchanging. While the world can redefine what truth is in a moment, God's Word has stood unchanged for over 2000 years.

I want to encourage you to embrace the fire when God places it before you. It is intended to refine and loosen. It was in the fire that Shadrach, Meshach, and Abednego met the Lord face-to-face. It is the place where they were freed from their chains. It was the place where they were delivered. The Lord can use the fire as your place of deliverance, but it will never happen if you're unwilling to admit the truth, especially before others.

I want you to take some time to invite the Holy Spirit to search your heart and for you to ask two questions:

1. Lord, am I standing on the truth of Your Word alone?
2. If not, will you show me how?

CHAPTER SEVEN: Healing

He said, "If you listen carefully to the Lord your God and do what is right in his eyes, if you pay attention to His commands and keep all His decrees, I will not bring on you any of the diseases I brought on the Egyptians, for I am the Lord, who heals you."
Exodus 15:26, NIV

I hope I always remember the women's conference I went to in 2023. It was at Seacoast Church in Charleston, South Carolina. The Holy Spirit performed many miracles, but one of the most memorable was watching someone receive physical healing we had been praying for. Our Lord longs for us to catch the seed of healing, not just for ourselves, but for others. He wants us to have faith and a prayer life that believes He is still miraculously restoring people, bringing them from illness to health.

In a world that tries to quantify things, it can be hard to wrap our minds around this fruit. It can be difficult to really desire not only to be healed personally from our trauma and past wounds, but to stand in the gap as a prayer warrior and prophetically speak restoration to the body.

Simplistic Healing

We can overcomplicate healing, just as we do the rest of our lives. Or we can adopt a skeptical approach, considering that God may no longer be able to heal. We haven't seen it, so we don't believe it. Time and time again in scripture, Jesus heals people who are blind, possessed by demons, the sick, and even the dead. He does this with what appears to be an effortless nature. We never once see Jesus laboring to His Father to create a healing moment. We never see Him waver as to whether His Father will answer Him and heal. Jesus merely responds in each circumstance as the Holy Spirit prompts him.

Jesus' desire to heal all hinges on His heart for man. He longs to see them restored as He saw them in the garden. His heart aches for their hardship and suffering. Jesus' ministry was marked by healing, which points not only to the Father's ability to heal but also our inheritance as His children.

Jesus sharing the gift of healing with His disciples while He walked on the earth and after His resurrection indicates that He wants us to walk in the full authority of healing, believing that healing wasn't just something He DID, but something He STILL DOES.

As the disciples were sent out two by two to heal many who were sick, the power of God fell on them to perform miracles. But each of the disciples submitted to and obeyed Jesus's commands to go. They regarded Him as Lord, His word as true. Not once do we see a dialogue between Jesus and a disciple in which they ask,
"So what do I do if they aren't healed?"

The enemy stands to gain ground in this area because if he can get us to believe it's not real, it's an area of our faith and prayer life that we may never explore. We become passive in this area of our walk and ultimately say we don't fully believe God's Word—that He, the Lord of Lords, is limited. In reality, it is our hearts and minds that are blocked by barriers. We stand outside the gate, not moved to walk in because it has too much mystery. Yet, He's calling us from outside the gate to the inner courts. We often put the burden on ourselves as healers, instead of on Jehovah Rapha.

So, instead of possibly experiencing the hand of God miraculously, we settle for a lukewarm, predictable walk with God—unwilling to intercede for the needs right before us.

Following God does not guarantee that everything will work out perfectly from a human perspective. In fact, scripture would point us to quite the opposite conclusion. Following God is full of mystery and uncertainty, because as we are trying to figure things out, God is trying to get us to trust Him.

There is no way I can articulate and fully explain the truth or gift of healing. I don't think any person can. However, I can point us all back to the truth in the Word of God, as modeled by God, man, and Jesus Himself. Healing is part of our inheritance. God desires for us to believe it is still possible today.

You Don't Have to Agree With the Spirit

One of the hindrances to healing personally from past traumas and pains is our inability to disagree with and renounce the spirit harming us. We are waging war not just with feelings or emotions but with spirits: "For our struggle is not against flesh and blood, but against the rulers, against the authorities, against the powers of this dark world and against the spiritual forces of evil in the heavenly realms" (Ephesians 6:12, NIV).

It's possible to confess and desire to turn away from past ways of thinking, but still live a life that is stuck. We give the spirit authority as we come into agreement with or accept what it's saying.

When we struggle with feeling confident about ourselves, and we have a continual bully mindset telling us we aren't skinny enough or smart enough, we are coming alongside the lie of the enemy and unintentionally drive ourselves further down the tunnel of illusion. We can find ourselves grasping onto the feelings of disappointment, fear, worry, and betrayal because we believe it will hurt more to heal. The possibility of love or healing almost seems unfamiliar and unsafe, so we settle for bondage because we perceive, at least here, we won't get hurt again. The bondage is at least a familiar spirit, unlike freedom.

When we say "yes" to the lies of the enemy and submit to them, then they have power. We have to submit for them to take root. What worries or lies of the enemy have you been submitting to?

The quick practical tip: When I experience the enemy's taunts and a spirit I know is not of God, I will verbally acknowledge it: "This is not a spirit of God. I don't have to choose to accept this. I don't accept this." Then, I will take a moment to pray or merely try to anchor my mind on Christ and the Word. James tells us, "Submit yourselves, then, to God. Resist the devil, and he will flee from you (James 4:7, NIV).

Family Healing

Personal healing is so essential to the family unit as a whole. As parents, we get the unique opportunity to teach our kids how to live and how not to live. We all have memories of both, likely from our parents. There are things we seek to imitate with our spouses and stuff we are intentionally trying to avoid. How we heal in marriage hardships, friendship disagreements, past trauma from our childhood, and day-to-day life pains, gives our children a roadmap for which paths to take themselves. Regardless of how much we may try to shelter or protect our children, they will inevitably, like all humans, encounter situations in life that will require personal healing. If we train them always to appear as though they have it all together, healing will be seen as a weakness or something to be avoided. And they will, in private, have no tools to combat the enemy's attacks.

If we teach them that praying for healing for someone else is unnecessary because God doesn't do it anymore, we will raise children who go to God for basic necessities rather than for abundance. They will start believing and praying only for what is before their eyes.

The Lord is calling the heads of the family to train their children up in the way they should go. Not in the way they "should kind of go" or the way that "looks nice to go," but the way they "should go." There will be many alternative routes for you to train your children, but just because a route looks desirable doesn't mean it's beneficial. The family call is for the whole church body. If you're reading this and thinking, This doesn't apply to me because I don't have children, please be aware that it does. God has placed nieces, nephews, neighbors, and friends' kids in your life for a reason: to be a light to them, share Jesus with them, and listen to them.
One of the sweetest conversations I ever had with my nephew was when he shared with me an area of his life in which he was hurting,

unprompted and unexpected. He opened up willingly, we got to pray together, and it gave me something to continue to pray for him about. I spoke about my healing and, in a moment, was able to disciple my nephew. Many of these moments are waiting for us to step into.

God longs to co-labor with us to bring His miracles and power into the world. He doesn't need us to accomplish it, but He chooses to include us in it. Do you long for personal healing today? Take some time to pray over yourself, to allow the Holy Spirit to reveal any spirits not of God that you're coming into agreement with. May He show you anything that may be halting your healing.

Do you lack faith that God still heals physical bodies today and wants to use you to do it? Take some time to ask the Lord what's blocking your belief. He delights to prove Himself trustworthy.

"You unbelieving generation," Jesus replied, "how long shall I stay with you? How long shall I put up with you? Bring the boy to me." So they brought him. When the spirit saw Jesus, it immediately threw the boy into a convulsion. He fell to the ground and rolled around, foaming at the mouth.

Jesus asked the boy's father, "How long has he been like this?" "From childhood," he answered. "It has often thrown him into fire or water to kill him. But if you can do anything, take pity on us and help us." "'If you can'?" said Jesus. "Everything is possible for one who believes."

Immediately the boy's father exclaimed, "I do believe; help me overcome my unbelief!" When Jesus saw that a crowd was running to the scene, he rebuked the impure spirit. "You deaf and mute spirit," he said, "I command you, come out of him and never enter him again."
Mark 9:19-25, NIV

Fruit in the Field

CHAPTER EIGHT: Repentance

He went into all the country around the Jordan, preaching a baptism of repentance for the forgiveness of sins. As it is written in the book of the words of Isaiah the prophet:
A voice of one calling in the wilderness,
'Prepare the way for the Lord,
make straight paths for him.
Every valley shall be filled in,
every mountain and hill made low.
The crooked roads shall become straight,
the rough ways smooth.
And all people will see God's salvation.'
Luke 3:3-6, NIV

<u>Repentance Isn't Just Saying Sorry</u>

At the command of the Lord, John begins to prepare the way for the Messiah. The process doesn't include preparing an event venue, setting up lights, or bringing fine garments to clothe Him in. The preparation for the Messiah is a call to repentance. Repentance will precede the second coming of Jesus, as it did the first time with John. Repentance is a fruit cultivated in humility and submission. It is born out of our deep awareness of our need for the blood of Jesus. We need to repent continually because our sin contaminates that which is pure.

God called John the Baptist to lay the foundation for the King of Kings, and His cry was far different from what many could have imagined. It wasn't about pointing fingers at others, but about an inward look at ourselves to see our need for cleansing and returning to the Lord. Repentance, when regularly lived out and exercised, cultivates not just a closer, more intimate relationship with the Father but also brings nutrients to the soil to be able to birth other fruit more easily. When we submit to turning from our sins, we become more fruitful in every area of our lives.

Repentance is a daily heart posture that allows the Holy Spirit to correct and guide us according to the Word of God. It helps us to actively turn away from sin and instead turn to God's way. It's not just the action of confession; it's the active lifestyle of learning to live according to the Holy Spirit's guidance, moment by moment.

Before Jesus saved us, we lived a life independent of Him. We made decisions and choices based on what we desired or perceived to be right. But after we gave our lives to Jesus, scripture tells us we are to "put off the old self which belongs to your former manner of life and is corrupt through deceitful desires, and to be renewed in the spirit of your minds, and to put on the new self, created after the likeness of God in true righteousness and holiness" (Ephesians 4:22-24).

Thus, we are no longer the guides of our lives, but the Lord Himself is. To repent means to rearrange your entire way of thinking, feeling, and being to forsake that which is wrong.[2] And the only way we can do that is with the Holy Spirit's guidance in our daily lives.

<u>Repentance is a Daily Posture</u>

Produce fruit in keeping with repentance. And do not think you can say to yourselves, 'We have Abraham as our father.' I tell you that out of these stones God can raise up children for Abraham. The ax is already at the root of the trees, and every tree that does not produce good fruit will be cut down and thrown into the fire.

I baptize you with water for repentance. But after me comes one who is more powerful than I, whose sandals I am not worthy to carry. He will baptize you with the Holy Spirit and fire.
Matthew 3:8-11, NIV

John is making it very clear that to avoid being chopped down, you must produce fruit. He urges us to continue producing the fruit of repentance, thus not retreating or disengaging, but maintaining a continual posture of repentance. As a fruit tree grows, it needs constant watering and care. There is a time to prune the branches and a time to fertilize. There is a continuous process of care necessary to produce fruit. If one is to neglect a fruit tree, it may bear some fruit, but not as much as it optimally can.

The continual care of the tree yields healthier, more abundant fruit. Repentance is a constant process. There is not a day that passes that we should not be exercising the fruit of repentance. There can be waves of repentance in our lives: times when we are going through hardship, times of refining, or times of celebrating a significant moment in Jesus' life (i.e., Easter, the day of atonement, Christmas). This is where repentance becomes more prevalent in our hearts and minds. However, repentance is a daily posture we are to maintain as believers in Jesus, not just in specific seasons. Repentance not only refines us, but it also makes us more Christ-like.

Are You Confessing or Repenting?

One of the misunderstandings we can have about repentance is that it's merely apologizing or recognizing our sins. While confession is biblical and necessary, confession and repentance are two different things. To repent is to turn from the sinful behavior or pattern you have confessed to. If I tend to be gluttonous and admit it, but never change how I eat, I'm not truly repentant. Repentance is active, not passive.

I once heard a Pastor say the fruit of repentance can't be seen instantly, but months or years later. We can be deceived into thinking we are repentant when, in fact, we are just great at confession. We confess our sins to others and God, but continue to walk in the same manner as before, never turning or redirecting our steps. If our actions never change, then we are not actually repentant in heart. We are merely doing what we think is "right."

God exposes and shows us things to repent for with the intention of drawing us closer to Him. He does this by exposing sin and giving us freedom. That's it—there's no hidden strings attached to it. Repentance is one of the most intimate things we can experience between us and the Father. It reveals our weaknesses and failures, yet unlike people who may have turned away from us in such moments, God responds with love, extending His arms toward us. This is the very essence of agape love.

There is no sin able to withhold us from the love of our Father. We are the only ones who can turn from His love, grace, and mercy. May you live a life where repentance is the longing of your heart because you're FULLY KNOWN, not needing to hide from the One who knit you together.

CHAPTER NINE: Patience

At that time the kingdom of heaven will be like ten virgins who took their lamps and went out to meet the bridegroom. Five of them were foolish and five were wise. The foolish ones took their lamps but did not take any oil with them. The wise ones, however, took oil in jars along with their lamps. The bridegroom was a long time in coming, and they all became drowsy and fell asleep.
At midnight the cry rang out: 'Here's the bridegroom! Come out to meet him!' "Then all the virgins woke up and trimmed their lamps. The foolish ones said to the wise, 'Give us some of your oil; our lamps are going out.'

'No,' they replied, 'there may not be enough for both us and you. Instead, go to those who sell oil and buy some for yourselves.' "But while they were on their way to buy the oil, the bridegroom arrived. The virgins who were ready went in with him to the wedding banquet. And the door was shut.

Later the others also came. 'Lord, Lord,' they said, 'open the door for us!' But he replied, 'Truly I tell you, I don't know you.' Therefore keep watch, because you do not know the day or the hour.
Matthew 25:1-13, NIV

Patience is the capacity to tolerate challenges or delays without getting upset.[3] While patience is not something many of us would admit is a strength, it is a necessary fruit for a believer. In fact, it could be one of the fruits we more easily overlook or merely label as a character flaw: "I'm just not a patient person."

Jesus' ministry and life echo the fruit of patience. Even though He was aware He had come to redeem the world, He waited patiently for His Father's timing to begin preaching the good news of the

Gospel. He was not eager to jump ahead or rush into what He had been commissioned to do. He submitted to earthly parents, worked as a woodworker, and lived a humble and meek life. Even when Jesus stepped into His ministry, He was never in a hurry to rush out of an interaction with a person or an opportunity.

The fruit of patience is so lacking in our society today. It's no wonder that even as believers in Jesus Christ, we can find ourselves struggling to see the fruit of patience cultivated in our lives. Our culture can deliver almost anything within a quick window. With demands for instant gratification on the rise, we are called to a lifestyle of patience as we bear the image of Jesus.

Prepared to Wait

In the parable of the Ten Virgins, a stark difference is evident in the behavior of these ten bridesmaids. Half have brought extra oil, and half have not. As they wait for the bridegroom's arrival, half find out they haven't prepared adequately. The five have come with no extra oil reserve; they haven't planned to wait, to be patient. They planned for the bridegroom to arrive quickly, in their timing.

Our Lord will return again, as the Word of God teaches. We are currently waiting for Jesus's second coming. While we are waiting for His return, can I ask you how you're waiting? Are you waiting, focused on receiving for yourself what you desire in the flesh? Or are you looking to eternity with eyes locked on having an oil reserve for His coming? While we are often slow to wait for things in our life to come to pass (marriages, kids, jobs, opportunities), we are quick to forget the one thing we are to be eagerly expecting, with patience—Christ's return.

The five wise bridesmaids not only brought extra oil, indicating more labor, forethought, and preparation, but they also demonstrated through their actions a devotion to their bridegroom. The thought of not having what was necessary for his arrival, regardless of the wait time, was not an option for them. They came prepared to wait.

They were prepared for his timing rather than their own timing. The extra oil present was an awareness in heart and mind that waiting was not an obstacle for them, but a delight. They longed so badly to be with the bridegroom that they wouldn't let a lack of forethought or discipline slip by.

Are you prepared to wait for your bridegroom today? When we patiently wait for His return, focusing on His splendor, our priorities in life begin to shift. What once was something we desired falls to the wayside because it's not something that will stand the Fire of Heaven in eternity.

It is a joy to wait for the return of our Savior; to look to the clouds for His white horse and robe dipped in blood. We are often laboring, working, and striving in vain for things that only steal our patience and peace, and ultimately redirect our eyes and focus to things not of the Lord. We lose the gift of waiting with expectant eyes and full jars of oil for our bridegroom.

What if patience was not merely about an outward transformation in action or an inward shift of heart, but about Christ Himself? What if we viewed patience as a way to prepare for Christ's return?

Pride Inhibits Fruit

The biggest inhibitor to patience is pride. We will discuss this in more depth in a couple of chapters, but it's valuable to know that if you're struggling to see the fruit of patience in your life, it's likely that pride is bearing fruit instead. Pride says, "I'm being inconvenienced, thus I'm not patient." Pride says, "If only these kids would behave, then I wouldn't have to yell." Pride says, "Why hasn't God responded to what I asked of him?" Pride says, "I deserve to be upset." While we desire to experience a gracious and patient God, we often struggle to extend the same attributes to the people around us.

The Word of God is littered with the fruit of patience and the consequences of pride. The Bible is full of men and women who chose to wait on God. And in the process of waiting patiently, God developed values, character, and resilience in them for the road ahead. In the Old Testament, Jacob had to wait for Rachel. Joshua had to wait until Moses and those who left Egypt all died before entering the Promised Land. We see Ruth waiting on Boaz. After her fast, Esther had to wait to talk to her husband about her people. David had to wait for the throne. Job had to wait for healing. Jesus had to wait to step into His ministry. The disciples had to wait for the Holy Spirit at Pentecost.

Patience is a fruit that's hard to cultivate in large quantities. It often dies in most people's soil because they lack the nutrients needed for patience to flourish. The soil for patience needs to contain selflessness, trust in God, and a hunger for God's will in your life.

It's hard to be patient when everything revolves around your desires and will. Trusting in God is crucial because if you don't trust Him, you won't wait on Him. A hunger for God is the thing that will keep you in the spot that He has asked you to stay in, even if it's taking too long, even if it doesn't make sense. Even if . . .

Introduction to Part II:
The Struggle to Keep Going

When you hear the word bad, what comes to mind? Is it something you saw, something you did, is it a person, a movie, a song you heard on the radio, or something else? I ask this because we are about to delve into a section of this book that highlights the bad fruit in our lives. It's the part that you likely want to skip over. The part you feel less than excited to read. But before you decide to sign off and throw this book on the shelf with the other half-read books in your house, give me just a few pages to try and convince you otherwise. I'll let you decide at the end.

God has used some bad situations to still bless and prosper His people time and time again in the Bible. God blessed the Israelites, even in their disobedience, with water and food. God still allowed David to be King and gave him another son, even after he killed Uriah and stole his wife Bathsheba. God still used Samson to destroy the Philistines, even though he'd given in to his own lust. God still used Peter as the rock on which He built His church, even though He denied Jesus three times. God still used Paul even though He had persecuted and killed many followers of Jesus. God still wants to use you and me even though _________________________.

There is wisdom in being exposed to our areas of sin, failure, and weakness. There is insight in looking at the ugly part of our hearts that we've allowed to go unaddressed. Bad fruit is merely fruit that does not align with the will or desire of our Father. It is a fruit that creates division, separation, and spiritual attacks that Satan himself hones. While God can redeem our past mistakes, He is calling us to a holier way of living, where only His fruit stands.

Some of the fruit I live in today is because of my choice to remove bad fruit from one season and recultivate the land. The field, once littered with belief and unbelief, legalism and faith, love, and hatred, is being cleared so that only the fruit that comes from the Word of God stands.

It's hard to change what is still masked and veiled, which is why I felt prompted by the Lord to write these chapters ahead. Being ignorant of how the enemy is luring and distracting us is irresponsible. There are only six bad fruits that the Spirit gave me insight into, but there are many more.

I urge you not to be afraid to look at the overgrown field. Do not be afraid to take some time to allow the Spirit to guide you in identifying areas where you can make adjustments. Without assessing our bad fruit, what is good can be choked out by thorns and weeds.

I'll leave you with this, my last-ditch effort to encourage you to read on. When my husband and I first got married, one of the things we decided to do was take Dave Ramsey's "Financial Peace" course. It was a class offered at my job. They say every marriage usually has a saver and a spender. Ours met that quote. My husband raved about the class, so I said, "Yes." Let me be clear, I didn't want to go, but I thought this would be good for our marriage.

I didn't want to go because I didn't want to hear that I needed to change something. I didn't want healthy boundaries imposed on me because they felt like limitations; I wanted to spend as I'd spent. "I deserved it," was the soundtrack playing in my head. The class lasted approximately 8 weeks, and each session built upon the previous one. Can I tell you that week 3 really ruffled my feathers when Dave recommended a 3-6 month savings fund?

To do this, sacrifices had to be made. There were things I'd have to give up, and a tighter budget we'd have to stick to. More accountability and more responsibility. It was anything but what I wanted to hear. After completing the class, we did just that. We began to save for our 3-6 month emergency fund.

I'll tell you in complete transparency, there was a lack of financial accountability until the Lord exposed my bad fruit in finances through my husband's desire to take the class. The only way I was able to start to work on my bad financial habits was to look at them. I couldn't avoid them any longer. My husband, in his loving way, forced me to face it head-on and begin the process of uprooting it. Had I opted not to go to the class with my husband and continued my spending habits and ignorance, I can guarantee you we would have had many more fights. There would have been a spirit of hiding, shame, and condemnation when buying things, and likely we would have been in more financial debt.

I look back now, grateful for that hard-exposing season. It was hard to realize I was doing it all wrong. I was cultivating fruit that was not honoring God, my husband, and my family. God, in His kindness, didn't just change the habit; He exposed the mindset. Behind every bad piece of fruit is a mindset that Christ has not renewed.

I can't force you to take the next step, to turn the page. Only you can choose that. But what I can do is believe, as you read, the Spirit of God will both expose to you what needs to shift and clothe you with His love and acceptance.

Fruit in the Field

PART II

BAD FRUIT

Fruit in the Field

CHAPTER TEN: Deception

Make a tree good and its fruit will be good, or make a tree bad and its fruit will be bad, for a tree is recognized by its fruit. You brood of vipers, how can you who are evil say anything good? For the mouth speaks what the heart is full of. A good man brings good things out of the good stored up in him, and an evil man brings evil things out of the evil stored up in him.
Matthew 12:33-35, NIV

You belong to your father, the devil, and you want to carry out your father's desires. He was a murderer from the beginning, not holding to the truth, for there is no truth in him. When he lies, he speaks his native language, for he is a liar and the father of lies.
John 8:44, NIV

In Matthew and John, we see the same sentiment ringing true. The religious leaders had a fruit issue called deception. While the Torah was intended to correct and guide them, their hearts had grown hard, bitter, and legalistic. Their religious acts mimicked a lifestyle submitted to God, yet their true hearts and actions towards Jesus were the antithesis of this. When we think about deception, we often perceive it as something happening to us. And while it is possible for someone to deceive or mislead us, we can also mislead or deceive ourselves.

I want us to look at this chapter with open hearts, asking the Lord, "Is there anywhere I'm deceiving myself?" Or, "Is there anywhere I'm trying to deceive others?" Deception is something not outwardly apparent. Most often, it has a way of hiding itself. Many times throughout my life, the Holy Spirit has had to reveal where I was being deceived. While we would like to believe we can see deception a mile away, we can be quite gullible.

Please be encouraged that, as you ask, the Lord will likely reveal something. If we have the eyes to see it now, we will be able to deal with it. Let's not be like the religious leaders, portraying to others and ourselves a false righteousness that the truth cannot penetrate.

<u>Self-Righteousness</u>

The religious leaders who opposed Jesus in these instances perceived themselves as righteous, yet their actions were rooted in self-righteousness. Jesus wasn't just addressing their hearts; He was addressing the seed of self-righteousness within them. When we view ourselves as the final authority, we elevate ourselves to the status of our own god and are no longer teachable or submitted.

> *Do not deceive yourselves. If any of you think you are wise by the standards of this age, you should become "fools" so that you may become wise.*
> *1 Corinthians 3:18, NIV*

One of the areas that self-righteousness can bubble up from is the spirit of legalism. This is following what appears to be the words of God, but utilizing them to justify or purify yourself. The spirit of legalism is deadly because it gives the perception of life, but death is lurking beneath the surface. Often, the spirit of legalism is not only used as a measuring stick against oneself, but it is also improperly and harmfully used against others. Legalism can leave us measuring others up to a standard that is not true and assessing them with a lack of love, mercy, or grace.

The Lord is the only one with the authority to judge someone's heart. He is the only One who is pure, and He's the very One who created them. Yet, we can think we have the right to judge and hold people to standards out of a self-righteous and, at times, a legalistic spirit. That is not the way of God.

Satan desires to hide the truth from us. He wants to get us alone so we can figure it out all by ourselves. His deception tactic is merely self-reliance and logic from a worldly standpoint. As we follow this path, we begin to quantify and strategize rather than lean into the Spirit of God to lead us. Deception is not merely trickery from another; it is primarily done to ourselves by ourselves. I wonder how many of us are thinking something false about God that's making us operate in self-righteousness? All the while, we believe we are justified in our actions and that they are the best option, which, in and of itself, is an oxymoron. The best choice will always be whatever God speaks. Let us not be deceived into thinking otherwise.

Deceiving Others and Yourself

Do you, at times, try to present yourself a certain way before others? Do you downplay your faith in Christ to make others feel more comfortable? Do you tell your family and friends you're okay, even though inside you're falling apart?

These may have never struck you as examples of deception, but they are. They are false truths, deceiving actions, lies told, or thoughts to present oneself as better than another. The reason Jesus was so hard on those religious leaders, I believe, is that they represented the church to so many. They were considered a spiritual authority, something to be mimicked or followed. If they remained uncorrected, it would leave the impression that following the process was more important than following the Savior; that looking all put together was more important than asking the One who made you to put you back together.

Satan wants to deceive us into not only bearing the fruit of deception but also living a life where we never feel like we are enough. A life where we always have a measuring scale, not just with ourselves but with others. He wants the shell of ourselves to portray something different from what's on the inside. Could Jesus be saying to you and me, "Stop?" Stop trying to deceive Me and tell Me one thing when we both know it's not true. Could God be trying to get into a locked-up heart of yours that has been more comforted by your doubt and self-righteousness than by His Word?

Fruit in the Field

Deception has become a way of living. We need to ask the Holy Spirit to search our hearts and show us what is causing us to present a facade to others and ourselves. Jesus was offering a better way when He was talking to those religious leaders. We know they didn't decide to take it. Instead, they remained in their old ways of living and thinking, doubting He was the Messiah and inciting fear among their peers. We know Jesus had to die for our sins. But what if they believed He was the Messiah? They would have eagerly wanted to learn and listen to Him. Their hearts would have been challenged to change in ways Jesus hadn't even spoken about because of their proximity to Him. They would have turned from their sin and not remained in it. They would have had eternal union with Him, rather than separation.

> *Do not merely listen to the word, and so deceive yourselves. Do what it says.*
> *James 1:22, NIV*

You have a choice, just like they did: Keep deceiving others with this person you try to portray and keep fooling yourself with lies that you need to look or be a certain way, or you can choose to break away and allow the Spirit to examine your heart. Confess your sin, repent of the sin, and run towards Jesus. Deception will keep you bound for a lifetime, but the truth will set you free for eternity.

If we claim to be without sin, we deceive ourselves and the truth is not in us.
1 John 1:8, NIV

CHAPTER ELEVEN: Fear

For the Spirit God gave us does not make us timid, but gives us power, love and self-discipline.
2 Timothy 1:7, NIV

One of the most toxic fruits we can cultivate in our lives is the fruit of fear. It desires not only to hurt but also to paralyze us from the things God has called us to. Many, if not almost all, believers have at some point dealt with the spirit of fear. And while we would never admit to intentionally cultivating it, we can often come alongside its manipulative tactics with false mindsets. Fear can only operate because we have not experienced healing or the redemptive work of God in our hearts and minds. Fear operates on mistruths and lies. It takes a small seed of doubt and exploits it in many ways, until we are thinking that this must be the truth.

Wherever you see fear operating in your life, there is a lie you've believed about God underneath that needs healing. One of the most unsuspecting ways we cultivate a spirit of fear in our lives is by believing it is more comforting to remain unhealed than healed. "At least I know what to expect." The lie gives the impression of protection, but in actuality, it further solidifies our fruit of fear.

Our antidote to this fruit is the Truth of God, the Word. When it fills our hearts and heads, there is no room for the spirit of fear to operate. We are running to many things to try and heal or fix our fears, but the only One who can and will fully heal us is Jesus.

Before we move any further, I want to remind us what Jesus and God said over and over again in the Bible, "Do not fear; do not be afraid." Looking at what has enslaved and harmed us for years can feel difficult, but we aren't doing it alone. We are looking at it with

Fruit in the Field

Jesus by our side, the Holy Spirit moving within us, and God ruling on His throne above. The Lord is removing and revealing the bad fruit of fear in our lives, and He's doing it to set us free.

<u>Fear of the Lord</u>

We are called to fear the Lord, to have a Holy reverence for Him, and to tremble at the thought of His moving. While we are struggling to shake off the fear of man and the fear of lack in our lives, the Lord is beckoning us to have a fear of Him. I start with this because it is the only fear we are actually to possess in our lives—the only fear which leads to repentance and nearness with the Father.

The fear of the Lord is a heart posture that acknowledges God's power, authority, and nature. The fear of the Lord leads us to desire to follow His commands and His prompts in our everyday lives. The fear of the Lord forces us to holy repentance and awareness of our smallness in comparison to our mighty God. The fear of the Lord will always point us to God and create humility in our hearts. The fear of the Lord recognizes that God is not merely a friend but a King enthroned, with elders surrounding Him, and that He deserves the utmost respect and honor. His fear is covered with righteousness and glory. His fear leads to wisdom and understanding.

The fear of the Lord is the beginning of knowledge, but fools despise wisdom and instruction.
Proverbs 1:7, NIV

Satan's fear does the opposite. It leads to confusion and a lack of clarity. It is covered up with other false thoughts and deception. It desires to expose and exploit for the sake of evil. Satan wants us to think his definition of fear is the same as the Father's. He wants us to live a life of fear with our Father. He wants us to remain afraid that we aren't forgiven for the thing we did thirty years ago, so he still has wiggle room to warp our minds and transform our hearts.

The fear of the Lord leads to life. It allows us to lay down our lives fully and submit to His ways without trying to wrestle with God.

Where in your life do you lack the fear of the Lord?

Fear of Man

We can spend a lifetime trying to please people and end up at the end of it in deep regret of all we missed. Why? Because we were never created to please man.

> *So God created mankind in his own image,*
> *in the image of God he created them;*
> *male and female he created them.*
> Genesis 1:27, NIV

We were created in God's image: to look, sound, and be like Him. Our inner desire is to bear the image of our Father. However, one of the most common ways we experience fear is by trying to please humanity and bear their image. Whether it's our parents, friends, spouses, or bosses, we can live our whole lives bound to man's approval of us instead of God's. The fear of man will stop us from stepping out in faith, cause us to chase after things that will later enslave us, and ultimately lead to division and separation from the Father. We cannot please man and God. We must choose which we are to follow. This is why Jesus said you can't serve two masters. You will love one and hate the other (Matthew 6:24, NLT).

Even within the body of Christ, there is far too much fear of man. While we should be operating in the Spirit and with freedom, many of us are still prone to seeking affirmation from man rather than from God. We find ourselves operating from a place of competition or acceptance, salivating for man's approval because we are instantly gratified. Lacking the desire to be approved of in private with God.

The fear of man will always limit your boldness and faith in Christ Jesus. It will inwardly quiet the Holy Spirit's movement and eventually twist your mouth to fit what we perceive we should say, not what God is leading us to say. Only the Lord can help to remove the fear of man from your life. There's no self-help book or speaker who can release you from it. It only comes by the blood of Jesus and the work of the Holy Spirit in you. If you are struggling with the fear of man, take a moment to seek the Lord right now and ask Him who or what is driving it. He is delighted to talk to you.

<u>**Fear of Lack**</u>

Excess, Excess, Excess. We live in a country that enjoys having excess. Whether it's cars, finances, items in our homes, knowledge, or food, excess is a Western cultural norm. While it may be normal here, it is not the God way. While God desires to provide for us, as any good Father would, He does not want us to use what He has blessed us with as a tool to shut Him out.

As we receive more from God, it can become easy to get close-fisted or begin to play a tune in our minds that we "deserve" all we have been given. But God has called us, as believers, to be conduits of His blessings. He gives us things to carry for a season and pass off in another.

One of the biggest inhibitors to our generosity and a culprit of greed is the fear of lack.

The fear of lack will lead you to store up when God asks you to give. The Lord has invited some of you to give. He's been talking for weeks or possibly years, but you have refused to do so because you allow the fear of lack to rule in your life. Lack says, "You won't have enough. You will run out. Will God provide?" Many Christians will not graduate to a place where their lives are intertwined with the first command that Jesus gave to the religious leaders when questioned.

> *"Jesus replied: 'Love the Lord your God with all your heart and with all your soul and with all your mind.' This is the first and greatest commandment."*
> Matthew 22:37-38, NIV

We often think our life is in line with this command, but if we experience any fear of lack in our minds, it speaks to an area, if not multiple areas, where we do not trust God. Trust and love go hand in hand. As my trust in my husband abounds, so does my love. Love is not merely a feeling; it is more centrally an action.

Love is patient, love is kind. It does not envy, it does not boast, it is not proud. It does not dishonor others, it is not self-seeking, it is not easily angered, it keeps no record of wrongs. Love does not delight in evil but rejoices with the truth. It always protects, always trusts, always hopes, always perseveres.
1 Corinthians 13:4-7, NIV

God defines love as not being self-seeking, always protecting, and always trusting. When we carry the fear of lack, we are self-seeking, try to defend ourselves, and ultimately don't trust God as our provider. The fear of lack is a lie. It points us in the opposite direction of Biblical love and further makes us self-reliant. It causes us to trust in our ways and our plans as though they are higher than the Lord's. Is there any area in your life where you're experiencing the fear of lack? What is God calling you to do with it?

Backstage Fear

I once had a young woman prophesy over me, "God's given you a gift in communication. You are hiding behind shyness. You're saying you're shy, but fear is the real reason you're not moving forward."

I can tell you she was 100% right. The Lord had given me opportunities I'd cowered away from. I downplayed the gift, thinking it was humility or shyness. Up until that day, it's what I would have told you. But when she said it was fear, something came undone. Fear was masked behind what I thought were humility and shyness. There are backstage fears in our lives. Fear that is simply hidden, covered up by a beautiful stage set with curtains. On the surface, it presents itself as one thing —sometimes good things —but all the while, it is actually fear.

As we discussed in the previous chapter, deception is the enemy's tactic to throw us off his scent. It is to get us to focus on the wrong issues while causing us to wander further and further from the actual truth. The enemy longs to deceive us into thinking some of the things we are resisting or saying "no" to are out of humility, a desire to rest, or out of protection for us or our families financially. But in actuality, fear could be the spirit of deception lying beneath the surface.

You have been given authority through Christ if you've decided to follow Him. It doesn't have to be a public decision or one made on Sunday, but rather, it's one made between you and God. An open heart that acknowledges Jesus' life and death for your sins. He is the only way to the Father. If we stand in authority, friend, there is no reason why we should even be entertaining fear in our lives, nor should we allow it to bear fruit. You have power over the spirit of fear because of the Word of God. You can experience victory over the spirit of fear through the power found in Christ and His blood shed at Calvary.

What would it look like for more of God's people to be walking only in the Fear of the Lord? To be clothed in confidence and truth. Not in complacency, not in worry, not in anxiety, not in depression. I encourage you to fight for your field, to fight for your fruit. One day, someone will inherit our produce. May it be said of us that we broke off generational curses, one bad fruit at a time.

CHAPTER TWELVE: Pride

*For everything in the world—the lust of the flesh, the lust of the
eyes, and the pride of life—comes not from the Father
but from the world.*
1 John 3:16, NIV

Pride is arrogance. Pride thinks it knows better and is better. Pride
sets itself in first place. It bows to no one but itself. "Pride is spiritual
cancer: it eats up the very possibility of love, or contentment, or even
common sense."[4] We are currently elevating the word "pride" and
associating it with movements that contradict God's commands. In
society, it is deemed healthy to have pride in oneself or what we've
achieved in our own strength and power. But that's not the way of
the Lord. Pride is a fruit of the enemy.

The Heart

*To humans belong the plans of the heart,
but from the Lord comes the proper answer of the tongue.
All a person's ways seem pure to them,
but motives are weighed by the Lord.
Commit to the Lord whatever you do,
and he will establish your plans.
The Lord works out everything to its proper end—
even the wicked for a day of disaster.
The Lord detests all the proud of heart.
Be sure of this: They will not go unpunished.*
Proverbs 16:1-5, NIV

The dwelling place for the spirit of pride is the heart. Proverbs shows
us that in our hearts we plan and are proud. The contamination of
the pride of life is a heart issue. Pride thinks its ways are the best and
is motivated by self, not by God. But I'm so thankful that the Word
of God guides us to see the antidote to pride.

Fruit in the Field

"Commit to the Lord whatever you do, and He will establish your plans" (Proverbs 16:3). The key is submission: giving Him your WHOLE LIFE. You no longer make decisions apart from Him. Pride struggles to exist when we continually seek the Lord's voice and commit our ways to His plans.

If you were to be honest, where in your life are you not seeking God's ways or plans? Where are you still ruler and judge? Where are you not submitting?

The call to a life laid down for God is a mandate for all Christians, but few will walk the narrow path. Instead, many will live divided lives, operating in pride and self-reliance during the week and walking with God during set aside time slots. Many will struggle to step fully into the power or authority of Christ because pride is operating.

> *When pride comes, then comes disgrace, but with humility comes wisdom.*
> *Proverbs 11:22, NIV*

Choosing NOT to Love

The bad fruit of pride keeps us from obeying the two commandments Jesus gave us.

> *"'Love the Lord your God with all your heart and with all your soul and with all your mind.' This is the first and greatest commandment. And the second is like it: 'Love your neighbor as yourself.' All the Law and the Prophets hang on these two commandments."*
> Matthew 22:37-40, NIV

If we are living a life of chasing after things we desire while ignoring or silencing God's commands, we are not actually loving Him. To love God is to lay your life down in full. To love the Lord our

God with all our heart, soul, and mind means that everything is submitted to Him; there is not a single area of our life that we have control over. When we operate in the spirit of pride, we are actually waging war against God Himself. We do not love God rightly when we operate out of pride.

We are also not loving our neighbor. It's hard to love the one whom you are competing against, measuring yourself up against, or judging. Your mind will desire to tear down that person in private, only further to validate your "perceived worth." Thus, love is not a byproduct of this, but hatred, bitterness, and arrogance. Where in your life have you been measuring yourself up against your neighbor or coworker? Is there someone whom you have inwardly been murmuring about?

Pride is killing us from the inside out and drawing us further and further away from the commands of God. We must be aware that if the seeds of pride are growing in us, the seeds of love and humility are dying.

> *Pride goes before destruction, a haughty spirit before a fall. Better to live humbly with the poor than to share plunder with the proud.*
> *Proverbs 16:18-19, NIV*

The only way to deal with the fruit of pride is to bring it before God, allowing the Holy Spirit to expose and reveal what needs to be corrected. The fruit of pride must be pulled out and burned. There can be no room in us for entertaining it. It is a defiling fruit that will kill our relationship with Christ, try to sit on the throne of our hearts, and ultimately take over the field.

> *Do not plant two kinds of seed in your vineyard; if you do, not only the crops you plant but also the fruit of the vineyard will be defiled.*
> Deuteronomy 22:9, NIV

Fruit in the Field

CHAPTER THIRTEEN: Bitterness

*Get rid of all bitterness, rage and anger, brawling and slander,
along with every form of malice. Be kind and compassionate to
one another, forgiving each other, just as in
Christ God forgave you.*
Ephesians 4:31-32, NIV

Bitterness is defined as anger and disappointment at being mistreated; resentment.[5] It's easy to become focused on our own desires, thoughts, experiences, and emotions. But the Word of God, the Truth, tells us to get rid of all bitterness and anything that could lead us down this path.

While many of the emotions we feel can fuel bitterness, we have to be careful not to allow the enemy to use them to negate the Word of God. Satan longs for us to pick up anger, frustration, disappointment, jealousy, rage, and discontentment. If we do, we will unknowingly give bitterness a foothold. Bitterness can easily ride on the cusp of disappointment or unmet expectations. Are there any areas in your life where you are struggling with bitterness? If so, there are likely some other things beneath the surface that create a favorable environment for the seed of bitterness to grow.

<u>**Every Evil Practice**</u>
*"But if you harbor bitter envy and selfish ambition in your hearts,
do not boast about it or deny the truth. Such "wisdom" does not
come down from Heaven but is earthly, unspiritual, demonic. For
where you have envy and selfish ambition, there you find disorder
and every evil practice.*
*But the wisdom that comes from Heaven is first of all pure; then
peace-loving, considerate, submissive, full of mercy and good fruit,
impartial and sincere."*
James 3:14-17, NIV

Fruit in the Field

James uses the word "bitter" in conjunction with envy and selfish ambition, linking the two to paint a vivid picture. James tells us that where you find envy and selfish ambition, you find disorder and EVERY evil practice. He doesn't list a few evil practices, but says EVERY evil practice. Bitterness will drive us to do some sinful things, not just in action but in the heart. It will cause us to stop praying for someone, seek to intentionally hurt another, or overtly ignore the Word of God, all the while justifying our actions.

James defines bitterness, envy, and selfish ambition as an earthly "wisdom." In contrast, heavenly wisdom is first of all pure, then peace-loving, considerate, submissive, full of mercy, good fruit, impartiality, and sincerity. When we live with the rotten fruit of bitterness, we are given a strategy via James—first, purity. Bitterness despises purity because purity is rooted in Jesus. Purity does not consult emotions or experiences; purity calls out that which is out of alignment.

We can desire desperately to run from truth and purity when bitterness is present. I'm not sure if you've ever found yourself not wanting to read the Bible or seek wise counsel during seasons when your heart was bitter. Why not? Because the Truth, the purity of the Word, washes us. It exposes our sinful nature and does not seek to point a finger unless it's to Jesus as our example and guide. We can be offended at times that we are not able to wallow in our own self-inflicted wounds or others' inflicted injuries. It's as though we want to show everyone the pain rather than allow the Healer to patch it up. Where in your life do you need the healing touch of the Lord? Where have you been wallowing and allowing EVERY kind of evil access? Purity is the balm to the wound of bitterness. We need it desperately.

A Mouth FULL of Bitterness

> *"Their mouths are full of cursing and bitterness."*
> Romans 3:14, NIV

Over and over again, scripture speaks to the importance of what comes from our mouths. The Bible tells us life and death are in the power of the tongue, and what comes out of the mouth defiles us (Proverbs 18:21). To defile means to contaminate or to make something unholy. When bitterness begins to appear or take root, it seeks to spread lies about others and God. These lies never have to be articulated by our tongues, while they often are. These lies can merely ruminate in our minds, building strongholds.

Bitterness manipulates situations we have gone through or are enduring, leading us to write a pessimistic script in our hearts and heads, speaking to an unjust or unmerciful God or to evil, corrupt people. And while what happened to us may, in fact, have been evil (sin), an action alone does not fully define a person. Most especially, it does not define a believer in Jesus Christ. God is always at work writing a redemptive story in our lives.

When our mouths open and spew out death, which is anything against the will and Word of God, it is something that has been sitting in our hearts. It's an expression of a wrong belief we've clung to or a lie we've believed. Our mouths are among the most neglected areas of our lives, often left unchecked or unmanaged.

"Out of the same mouth comes praise and cursing. My brothers and sisters, this should not be."
James 3:10, NIV

At ALL times, it's important what comes out of our mouths. It is essential during testing, trials, or when bitterness is at hand. When the spirit of bitterness is trying to take root in our hearts, our tactic is to fight the lies with truth. I know it is easier said than done, but the more we exercise this, the more routine it will become. Our battle strategy isn't to give in to our emotions or even experience. Our approach is to take on the fruit of the Spirit, extending love and kindness to the very ones the enemy is trying to get us to retaliate against.

Satan wants us to be impulsive and to follow our feelings. When we do, he can create greater separation and cause harm to us and those we love. Our mouth is our most excellent well of life. We must be on guard not to use this well as a double-edged sword, spewing both freshwater and saltwater.

<u>Warning Signs</u>

Whenever bitterness is trying to take root, there may be some silent tendencies occurring in you, revealing warning signs. For example:

- You may pull away from someone or become silent in your frustration, slowly allowing bitterness to grow.
- You may over-discipline your child in a situation because you're upset from past mistakes they made, slowly allowing bitterness to grow.
- You may not be returning your friend or sister's call because of your belief that they think they're better than you, slowly allowing bitterness room to grow.
- You may be speaking poorly of a person who is more successful than you because you lust after what they have, slowly allowing bitterness to grow.

"We demolish arguments and every pretension that sets itself up against the knowledge of God, and we take captive every thought to make it obedient to Christ."
2 Corinthians 10:5, NIV

We stop bitterness by taking the thought captive and making it obedient to Christ. Warning signs signal that our thoughts are off the mark and that we are starting down a slippery slope if we do not immediately take these thoughts captive. Warning signs often stem from our emotions, past experiences, or thoughts, yet they consistently pull us away from loving God and our neighbor.

If the emotion is saying don't talk, speak. As we renew our minds to the Mind of Christ, we have to start making different decisions. As soon as we start seeing the warning signs of bitterness, we must lock up our minds like a vault, not allowing anything to enter.

Trying to live a life with a renewed mind that can spot bitterness and every kind of evil will take training and discipline. Bitterness is a secretive fruit. It lingers alongside other evil practices, seeking a way into our hearts, minds, and mouths. But we can shut it down and stop it. We use the Word of God as our guide and guard, allowing it not only to search us but also to point us to holiness and purity. Don't let bitterness in. Don't let bitterness in. Please, don't let bitterness in.

Fruit in the Field

CHAPTER FOURTEEN: Comfort

"But the Comforter, which is the Holy Ghost, whom the Father will send in my name, he shall teach you all things, and bring all things to your remembrance, whatsoever I have said unto you."
John 14:26, KJV

When Jesus ascended into Heaven, He told His disciples to wait for the promised gift of the Holy Spirit. While the Holy Spirit has many names, the one John mentions in the passage above is the Comforter.

If we were to assess our lives, we would likely find that many of our decisions are made out of a sense of comfort. When we rely on our own knowledge, understanding, and experience to make comforting decisions, we negate the gift of the Holy Spirit to fill this role.

Comfort seeks protection, consistency, and routines. Comfort looks out for self. It aims to create boundaries deemed "safe," all the while keeping us hostage to not truly relying on God. Comfort comes from the decisions we make instinctively, driven by familiarity. Comfort comes from the groups of people we choose to hang out with that share similar interests.

Comfort is killing our ability to step out onto the water and walk to Jesus. We are unwilling to leave our boats and our fish behind because it would feel uncomfortable to just follow God without a plan or explanation. Comfort is causing us to store up when God's desire is for us to hand out.

Financial Comfort

And He told them this parable: "The ground of a certain rich man yielded an abundant harvest. He thought to himself, 'What shall I do? I have no place to store my crops.'

Fruit in the Field

Then he said, 'This is what I'll do. I will tear down my barns and build bigger ones, and there I will store my surplus grain. And I'll say to myself, 'You have plenty of grain laid up for many years. Take life easy; eat, drink and be merry.'

But God said to him, 'You fool! This very night your life will be demanded from you. Then who will get what you have prepared for yourself? This is how it will be with whoever stores up things for themselves but is not rich toward God.'"
Luke 12:16-21, NIV

One of the most evident comforts of this world is money. It's a place many of us find our security and safety. When finances are sound or when we can buy the things we desire, then we feel comfortable. We have unknowingly allowed the comfort of money to control many of our life decisions.

This man, who was blessed with an abundance of crops, sounds much like our world today. Instead of asking God if there's something He wants him to do with the abundance, he keeps it for himself. By not seeking God's purpose for his abundance, he chooses to build a bigger barn, valuing comfort over embracing God's generous heart.

The comforts of this world will scream, *Store up for yourself, You worked hard for that, This is the wise way to spend your money*, and so many other narratives. In the Old Testament, God said not to go over your fields again after harvesting them and to leave the outside of the fields for the poor and the foreigner (Leviticus 19:9-10). The desire was not for the person to store the blessing, but to share it.

When we fight for financial comfort, it not only makes us stingy but also dries up the avenues God is trying to use to meet others' needs. Having money is not bad. But I once heard Bill Johnson say, "Too much money is the amount of money you have that causes you to stop relying on God."[6] Any area of our life where we begin to rely less on God and more on ourselves can become an area of comfort.

Physical Comfort

Now I want you to know, brothers and sisters, that what has happened to me has actually served to advance the gospel. As a result, it has become clear throughout the whole palace guard and to everyone else that I am in chains for Christ.
Philippians 1:12-13, NIV

Operating in a state of physical comfort is something we face daily. But our physical comforts will eventually be tested if we desire to walk in submission to God and His will for our lives. It is impossible to live a Christian life without laying down the idol of physical comfort. When we are striving for comfort, we are operating in the flesh and not the spirit. We desire to do what feels or appears gratifying to us rather than trust God. In doing this, we can halt or slow our sanctification process and merely settle for a lesser relationship with Christ, becoming dependent on physical comfort rather than on God. But if we are committed to laying down our lives, picking up our cross, and following Him, we will be forced to address the issue of physical comfort.

I love this passage of scripture with Paul. He is chained and in jail, rejoicing and praising the Lord. He is not viewing his physical discomfort or circumstances as a barrier or something to resent, but rather as a means to strengthen the body as a whole. He desires to fulfill the Will of God and make His name known, even behind bars.

If we want to be used mightily by the Lord, we will inevitably face physical discomfort. It may not look like jail, but it could look like moving somewhere He's calling you to. It could look like ministering to the hurting and homeless who most people walk by. It could look like going to church, even when it's the place where you feel hurt. It could look like walking through a sickness that is unexplained or incurable.
Jesus, over and over again, laid down His physical comfort to serve the Will of the Father. In our world, it's increasingly possible to live

comfortably but unchanged, to live stuck spiritually and in bondage. Comfort does not desire for us to grow with the Lord. Instead, it desires that we cling to ourselves. Our desire should not be to seek comfort in this world. Our desire should be to preach the Good News of Christ Jesus and to rejoice in the process, even during hardship.

<u>Testimony</u>

One of the most challenging years of my life tested not only my comfort but also my faith. My family and I had just moved to Charleston, South Carolina, and I was pregnant with our son. We moved on a Word from God, not knowing anyone. During this season, the Lord, in His kindness, began to remove the pillars I had come to lean on for comfort and security. People, places, and mindsets began to crumble. In the process, fear and other things I had struggled with began to surface.

As I ran from side to side, internally trying to find comfort in something I could lean on, nothing was found. All along, God had desired for me to find comfort in Him alone. In the midst of my life, I found ways to cope by leaning on other, more physical things. It was the Lord's kindness that led me to the testing season, to the wilderness. He led me there to free me.

There is freedom on the other side of dying to your comfort. There is true joy and gratitude. This is how Paul could have celebrated in his jail cell because he was not leaning on any false pillars. He was just as free in prison as he was unchained. It was a spiritual posture in which the Lord was as much his comforter and friend in jail as when he preached in the temple.

God is calling His Bride, the church, to find our comfort only in Him, not in our finances, friendships, spouses, families, neighborhoods, or other false pillars. Those things are gifts He's given us to enjoy. But they can't support, comfort, or draw near to us like the Lord. He longs to be our Comforter if we allow Him to be.

CHAPTER FIFTEEN: Coveting

You shall not covet your neighbor's house. You shall not covet your neighbor's wife, or his male or female servant, his ox or donkey, or anything that belongs to your neighbor.
Exodus 20:17, NIV

When we find ourselves coveting things in our lives, we are accepting and elevating something other than God on the throne of our hearts. We are willfully choosing to run after our desires rather than God's.

One of our most significant causes of jealousy is coveting what God has given to another. We covet when we desire what someone else has. We lust after their following, intimacy with God, spiritual gifts, possessions, finances, community, or influence. We begin to covet things of this world instead of loving God.

In today's society, it is easy to find oneself slipping down the slope of comparison. In a world that is highly focused on self and what one knows or owns, covetousness is among the most toxic fruits we encounter daily.

When God was establishing the law for His chosen people, He gave Moses a list of the Ten Commandments on Mount Sinai. The last of the commandments says, "You shall not covet your neighbor's house. You shall not covet your neighbor's wife, or his male or female servant, his ox or donkey, or anything that belongs to your neighbor" (Exodus 20:17). God clearly warns us to be on guard against our hearts' coveting. He tells Moses and the Israelites that if they covet what their neighbor has, it will only lead to separation between them, their neighbor, and the Father. When we covet, it becomes more challenging to see our blessings and what God has individually gifted us with, because we become hyper-focused on what we perceive we lack. The commands of God still ring true today and are beautiful guardrails for our lives. God's commands serve to keep us from harm or harming those we love. We are called, as believers of Jesus Christ, to follow the decrees and laws of our God. We will be held accountable for those actions that we did not choose to follow.

> *And this is love: that we walk in obedience to his commands.*
> 2 John 1:6, NIV

Coveting Beauty

> *Do you not know that your bodies are temples of the Holy Spirit, who is in you, whom you have received from God? You are not your own; you were bought at a price. Therefore honor God with your bodies.*
> 1 Corinthians 6:19-20, NIV

Our bodies are temples to the Lord. God created them for a purpose. And that purpose has everything to do with honoring Him and bringing glory to His name. We are called to care for and feed our temple with life-giving nutrients. These nutrients aren't merely part of a healthy diet; they're also how we care for our bodies spiritually, physically, and emotionally.

In our society, physical image and beauty are two of the most coveted things we encounter daily. Instead of finding gratitude and contentment in the bodies God has given us, men and women strive to attain a perfected, unwrinkled, not gray version of themselves. Going under knives and needles to stop or correct what society deems as signs of aging. This area of covetousness has built an industry around itself.

With plastic surgeons, lip injections, facials, hair colorists, the makeup industry, weight loss pills, and supplements, the underlying tone of this is that you are not enough, and what God has created is not good. We are walking around in shells that are idols we've erected, looking like a distorted image of what God created. We have coveted pants size, muscle mass, breast augmentations, and appearance. Are we possibly spending more time worrying about our appearance and body than we are about reading our Bible or thinking about the spotless Lamb of God?

The covetousness of the flesh has become more and more condoned and is not even seen as sin. But God in the Garden made Adam and Eve and said they were VERY good. He didn't say they needed editing or changing, but instead, He said they were "VERY good," just as He had formed them.

Then God said, 'Let us make mankind in our image, in our likeness, so that they may rule over the fish in the sea and the birds in the sky, over the livestock and all the wild animals, and over all the creatures that move along the ground.'

So God created mankind in his own image,
in the image of God he created them;
male and female he created them.
Genesis 1:26-28, NIV

God saw all that he had made, and it was very good. And there was evening, and there was morning—the sixth day.
Genesis 1:31, NIV

When we are slipping into a mindset that says we need to change parts of ourselves to be enough, better, or more attractive, it's a warning sign that somewhere our identity is not rooted in Christ. It's a warning signal that we covet appearance more than God Himself. Regardless of what we do to alter our bodies, they will all someday die and be resurrected, just as the Lord has said. I don't want to waste any more precious time on earth worrying about how my shell looks. As the Lord once spoke to me, "The body is merely the vessel for the Spirit. It gets the Spirit of God where it needs to be." How much more valuable are the contents inside the shell than the container?

Fruit in the Field

Where are you elevating the thought of owning or possessing something?

Where are you coveting beauty and appearance?

Where could you be operating in the lust of the flesh, the lust of the eyes, or the pride of life?

I'd like to lead you in a simple prayer to ask the Holy Spirit to reveal to you where you may be coveting things in your life.

Father, we come to you broken but valuable vessels. We thank you that our identity and worth are not found in our presentation before man, but in you alone. We ask for the Holy Spirit to reveal to us areas we are coveting things, we may not even be aware of. Help to renew our minds, reveal to us any wrong thinking, and free us from the bondage of our value coming through our appearance. May we walk as lights in a dark world, shining not because of our external appearance or possessions, but because of the Holy Spirit residing in us. Amen.

CHAPTER SIXTEEN: Conclusion

By their fruit you will recognize them. Do people pick grapes from thornbushes, or figs from thistles? Likewise, every good tree bears good fruit, but a bad tree bears bad fruit. A good tree cannot bear bad fruit, and a bad tree cannot bear good fruit. Every tree that does not bear good fruit is cut down and thrown into the fire. Thus, by their fruit you will recognize them.
Matthew 7:16-20, NIV

The fruit we bear in our lives is a reflection of our walk with the Lord. As our hearts and lives become more submitted to God's will and commands, we will inevitably see life-giving fruit spring forth. I hope that as you've milled through the pages, the Holy Spirit has shown you areas where you are cultivating good fruit. While good fruit is to be desired, we need not overcomplicate the process. As we remain connected to the vine, the Bible tells us we will bear fruit.

May we focus less on our branches and more on the vine. It can become easy to get so wrapped up in the appearance of full branches that we forget the One who waters, allows the sun to shine, and ultimately provides for the growth of the fruit in our lives.

May we also take heed. If we are to wander or drift from the author of life, our fields have the potential to become contaminated with bad fruit. Fruit that will distance and distract us from the Lord. Fruit that will try to silence the activity and voice of the Holy Spirit.

May we be recognized as good fruit, cultivated by proximity and relationship with the Father.

Lord, help us to be men and women who desire to follow your ways. May our lives bear good fruit in keeping with Your Holy Word. Help us

Fruit in the Field

to delight in the vine. And may we bear witness to Jesus in the process. Lord, guide us and awaken us to areas we are actively choosing to bear bad fruit or engage with it in others' lives. And help us rejoice in areas where You see the fruit of the Kingdom blossoming. May it bring you glory upon glory. Our lives are Yours, Lord. Amen.

APPENDIX

1. "Humility." Merriam-Webster.com Dictionary, Merriam-Webster, https://www.merriam-webster.com/dictionary/humility. Accessed 2 Jan. 2024.

2. Wieja, Estera. "What Did Jesus Mean by Repent? The Hebrew Meaning of Teshuva." FIRM Israel, January 18, 2023. https://firmisrael.org/learn/what-did-jesus-mean-by-repent-the-hebrew-meaning-of-teshuva/#:~:text=As%20seen%20in%20the%20story,more%20importantly%2C%20they%20showed%20transformation. simply.

3. "What the Bible Says about Patience." Bible Verses About Patience – Compassion International. Accessed January 16, 2024. https://www.compassion.com/christian-faith/bible-verses-about-patience.htm.

4. Fox, Christina. "What Is Pride?" Ligonier Ministries, June 7, 2023. https://www.ligonier.org/learn/articles/virtues-vices-pride.

5. "Oxford Languages and Google - English." Oxford Languages. Accessed March 12, 2025. https://languages.oup.com/google-dictionary-en/.jealousy.

6. Johnson, Bill. "How to Enter Your Promised Land and Leave behind the Wilderness - Bill Johnson Sermon, Bethel Church." YouTube, January 26, 2024. https://www.youtube.com/watch?v=OKR2w6k9vuQ&t=1105s.

Fruit in the Field